GEORGE BEST
TRIBUTE TO A LEGEND

# GEORGE BEST

## TRIBUTE TO A LEGEND

WEIDENFELD & NICOLSON

# Contents

'Don't coach him – he's a genius.'
 **Sir Matt Busby, 1961**

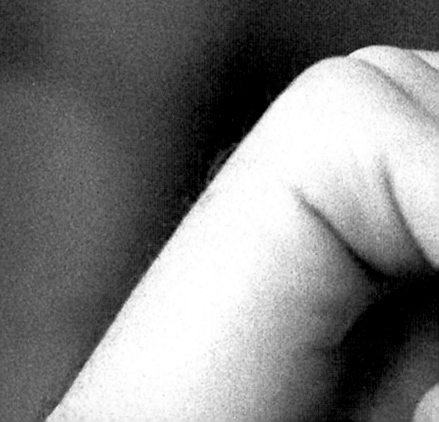

# Foreword

## By Sir Alex Ferguson

No matter your age, every Manchester United supporter, and a lot of other fans too, know all about George Best.

He was a player with an image that cuts through the decades and we all probably have a favourite memory. Even those who didn't actually see him play will have seen old film clips or heard about him.

George Best was a fantastic player and a tough character too, which he showed at the end of his life when he fought so long and hard to stay with us.

Any analysis of the world's greatest players is bound to include George Best. It's all about opinion of course, and everyone has their own idea, but you can be sure that the Irishman will figure high on everyone's list.

Some people say he didn't fulfil his potential at Manchester United because at 27 he started to go a little astray. But if you look at his record it's something like nearly 500 games and 200 goals, which is phenomenal considering he wasn't an out and out striker. What's more, he had an astonishing appearance record during the 10 years he played in the First Division. In five seasons he missed only nine League games, an incredible run, and he was pivotal in the European Cup victory over Benfica. So his contribution as far as Manchester United is concerned will be forever etched in the annals of the club's history.

He was such a special player, a phenomenal player, and I think I speak for everyone associated with Manchester United when I say he has left us with a million memories, all of them good ones, too. A footballer born with a mesmerising craft that left an indelible mark on people's lives.

I admired him as much for his courage as his talent. I can see him now, flying down the wing, riding tackles from defenders like Ron Harris, Tommy Smith and Norman Hunter. They were serious guys and you didn't mess with them, yet he rode all that. And when he was brought down he just got up again and looked for the ball even more eagerly. 'Give me the ball' was his message, and that will stick in my mind forever.

George Best arrived on the scene at a time when football was entering a certain post-war freedom. It was a liberated time with an explosion of music and fashion, and George became a part of that scene. He was different and became something football had not experienced before – a superstar. He was a marvellous, marvellous player.

A transfer fee for George nowadays? Impossible to define. I guess he would be priceless.

*Alex Ferguson*

**Story of a Legend**

**By David Meek**

## INTRODUCTION

Coming to terms with those shocking pictures of George Best, ravaged by illness as he lay at death's door, was difficult for those of us who remember the fleet-footed stripling who so mesmerised us with his football for Manchester United in the Swinging Sixties. Fifty-nine was far too early an age to leave us.

More and more, though, as time slips by, I know I shall recall a far different image of George. In fact I can see him now ... slim, boyish, dark hair shining in the floodlights as he scythes through the Benfica defence leaving a trail of baffled Portuguese defenders in his wake on his way to score the finest goal of the many, many I saw in 37 years reporting Manchester United for the *Manchester Evening News*.

It was sheer poetry as he swept from the halfway line to weave his way at speed past three white shirts before rounding goalkeeper Costa Pereira to clip the ball into the net. It was his second goal of the night and gave United an aggregate lead in their European Cup quarter-final against the most powerful team in Europe.

I can remember leaping to my feet, against all etiquette, in the Press Box, so stunning was that fluid scoring movement and so remarkable the circumstances. This was not a desperate last throw of the dice but a 19-year-old shadow of a boy from Belfast who with sheer, innate, feral talent made the world of football sit up and take notice. It was a *tour de force*, as audacious as it was unexpected, that changed the perception of the game.

From total domination in Europe, Benfica had been destroyed and you need look no further than the boy from Belfast for both the inspiration and the delivery of a performance that marked the introduction of George Best as a superstar, the game's first celebrity.

That, of course, was why it all unravelled. I am sure, though, that George would much prefer me and everyone else to remember him as the good-looking, fresh-faced boyo who took our game by storm one frenzied night in Lisbon.

He was undoubtedly touched by genius and he cut a vividly entertaining figure for a decade. Despite the drinking, a hectic love life, the liver transplant and marriage break-up, he remained immensely popular. People loved him as both a sublime player and a bad boy, perhaps because he cocked a snook at life itself as he pursued a lifestyle that was bound to catch up with him in the end.

But when you think about it, you realise that by the time he abandoned football and opted for a life with the reigning Miss Great Britain and his new night club, Slack Alice, George Best had more than paid his dues to the game. He might have left it young, but he started young: he played for 11 seasons in the First Division, packing more into his football career than the majority of professional players. If he had got into the first team at 21 and retired 11 years later at 32 nobody would have raised an eyebrow. George just happened to live his career a little sooner than most!

So when people say that he wasted his career they should remember that by the time he quit Old Trafford he had played 466 League, Cup and European games and scored 178 goals. We should also note that once he had established himself in the side he rarely missed a game. In fact in six of the seasons when he was in full flow he made either 40, 41 or 42 League appearances each year. And what a lot he had achieved – so many superlatives, and so many memories for us to savour. Those were magical years.

## LIKE A LITTLE JOCKEY

It was a story leaking out of the Manchester United training ground that first alerted me as the local evening paper correspondent that there was a special talent developing in the junior teams.

Harry Gregg, the experienced Northern Ireland international, volunteered to play with the juniors one afternoon at The Cliff training ground when one of the youngsters he later described as 'the skinny one' brought the ball up to him and scored by sending him diving the wrong way. Harry explains: 'A little later he wriggled clear again. I called his bluff and got the same result, a humiliating trip to terra firma with the ball at the other end of the goal. When George had the audacity to do it a third time I got up and joked: "You do that again and I'll break your bloody neck, son." I had a good laugh with George and the other lads. But when I left, the image of this pencil-thin lad with the breathtaking skills lingered on. Later that day I ran across Matt Busby at Old Trafford. We chatted briefly and as he turned to walk away I asked him if he had seen the youngster, the little Belfast lad. He hadn't, and I suggested he take a look. A few days later we met again. "I know the boy you mean. It's a pity he's so small," he said.' But those mesmerising skills he displayed that afternoon were to develop rapidly. Within two short years 'the skinny one' would be playing on the same team as Harry Gregg and a few seasons later hailed as one of the greatest players in world football.

*\*\**

As Mary Fullaway stood at the door of her house in Aycliffe Avenue in the Manchester suburb of Chorlton-cum-Hardy she could hardly have imagined she was welcoming the boy destined to become arguably the world's greatest footballer.

There he stood, her new lodger, along with another youngster straight off the boat from Belfast, Eric McMordie, to play for Manchester United. 'He looked more like a little jockey than a footballer. He was puny and he was petrified,' said Mrs Fullaway.

The two 15-year-olds were like fish out of water. McMordie was particularly homesick, and that night he persuaded George to go back to Ireland with him. So back they went. George's dad, Dickie Best, spoke with Matt Busby and between them they persuaded George to give it another go. Two weeks later he was back at Mrs Fullaway's sharing digs with David Sadler.

McMordie didn't return immediately but later joined Middlesbrough. There is no doubt George was quite overwhelmed by Manchester United. He found the other players intimidating and he was in awe of the first-team stars, like his hero Harry Gregg. 'I didn't know what to say to him,' said George, who still felt very shy in the company of others. He was isolated and alone but determined now to stick it out.

Little had happened in his life to prepare him for the ordeal of Manchester and life with a major football club. The Best family of two boys and four girls lived at Burren Way on the Cregagh housing estate. George was the eldest and his brother Ian was given the middle name Busby in tribute to Sir Matt.

There is a blue plaque now on the council house where they all lived. Not that George spent too much time there – he was always outdoors kicking a ball about.

Nobody, though, could see a future for him as a professional footballer. He was too lightly built, too thin and too small.

He passed his 11-plus at Nettlefield School but didn't like his senior school, Grosvenor High, because they played rugby. He played truant and was transferred to Lisnasharragh Intermediate. He played in the school team but it was at the local youth club where his football prospered. At Cregagh Youth Club he came under the tutelage of Hugh 'Bud' McFarlane who made the willing George one of his favourites. 'He was my boy at the club. If I wanted a message delivering I just called on George and off he went, taking a ball out of his pocket and dribbling it all the way there and back,' says Bud.

He was keen but despite his obvious skill his size was against him, certainly in terms of representative football. McFarlane thought he had a future, though, and in order to get him greater notice he arranged a match between his Under-15 youth club side and the Northern Ireland schoolboy team. 'We beat them 2-1. The idea was to put George on view and in my opinion he was the best forward on show.' The Irish schools selectors still considered him too light and small and the big club scouts all took the same line.

Plans were made accordingly for George to become an apprentice compositor in the *Belfast Telegraph* newspaper office. McFarlane tried one more time. He arranged a match so that Bob Bishop, United's legendary scout in Northern Ireland, could have a look at him. 'Bob was connected with another club that played in a different league so I arranged for Cregagh to play Bob's team, Boyland, and George scored two of the goals in a 4-2 win'. Bob apparently phoned Old Trafford chief scout Joe Armstrong to say he had struck gold!

Best went home to tell his dad: 'I think they are pulling my leg. Bud says there is an English club interested in me and I can go for a trial if I want.'

Nobody was kidding, though – the job at the *Belfast Telegraph* was abandoned and George duly took the boat to England to leave Cregagh Youth Club and spend the transfer fee … a £150 donation. Not a bad deal for Manchester United!

The boy still only stood 5 feet high and weighed a lightweight eight stone, but if United were worried about him growing and putting on a little more weight they were not left in any doubt about his skill. Not only was George's size held against him but he was also painfully shy. In his early days he used to walk the long way round to the dressing rooms to avoid meeting people.

He wasn't happy with his life outside training either. As a youngster from Ireland he was only allowed to come to England to play as an amateur, which meant he had to have a job and train part-time. So he was sent to work at the nearby Manchester Ship Canal offices because he had beautiful handwriting. But he was bored and wanted to be training with the other ground staff boys.

In the end the club found a friendly employer and sent George and John Fitzpatrick, another youngster in a similar situation from Scotland, to work for him. The arrangement was that they need only work in the afternoons, and so could train with the other lads in the mornings.

The lack of full-time training didn't seem much of a handicap, though, as he worked his way through the A and B teams, playing in the Lancashire League and making his mark in the youth team with an occasional game in the reserves.

Suddenly his career accelerated and four months after his 17th birthday and signing as a full-time professional he couldn't find his name on the team sheets for either of the junior teams, nor the reserves. He was playing for Manchester United – the big breakthrough, a first-team debut against West Bromwich Albion at Old Trafford on 14 September 1963. He performed well, giving the experienced full-back Graham Williams a torrid time. United won 1-0.

## HE WILL BRIGHTEN UP THE DULLEST OF GAMES

Just over 42 years later, on Wednesday 30 November 2005, Graham Williams and other members of the West Bromwich side of 1963 lined up on the pitch at Old Trafford to pay homage with a minute's silence to the man Sir Alex Ferguson described as 'a legend'. It was the first game at Old Trafford – Manchester United vs West Bromwich Albion – after George's death. Sir Alex Ferguson said in his welcome: 'A different time, a different era, but tonight I am sure both teams will be determined to honour the memory of George Best with what he did best, playing good football.'

***

Although he had already made up his mind to give him his League debut, Matt Busby put George down as a reserve for the First Division match against West Bromwich to spare him the ordeal of waiting. He needn't really have bothered with such niceties because, as George Best would demonstrate many times in the future, he was utterly nerveless. He may have been shy, even insecure, away from the pitch but on it he had a confidence bordering on the arrogant. He might have been reluctant to meet new people, unless they were attractive girls of course, but with a ball at his feet, he could talk in anybody's language.

He was played on the right wing and was up against Graham Williams, a rugged Welsh international full back. The game that marked his debut was not a classic affair but the Irishman made his mark and, without wishing to appear too much of a fortune-teller, this is what I wrote about him in my match report for the *Manchester Evening News*:

> There was also the prospect of young George Best to brighten up a dullish match. Despite the ordeal of a League debut after only three reserve matches, and a gruelling duel with full back Graham Williams, and a painful ankle injury, he played pluckily and finished the game in style.
>
> None of the handicaps could disguise a natural talent. I know manager Matt Busby is looking forward to seeing this Belfast boy in a team with Law to help him. I agree – it is an exciting prospect that will brighten up the dullest of games.

An accurate forecast of the future…

The game was won 1-0 with the scorer David Sadler, an England amateur at that time, who had shared digs with George in Chorlton. The team lined up: Gregg, Dunne, Cantwell, Crerand, Foulkes, Setters, Best, Stiles, Sadler, Chisnall and Charlton.

Best claims that the lasting impression of the game for him was how easy it had been, and that he was able to go out there and 'do the same things I'd been doing ever since I was a kid'. He reckoned it all came so naturally to him, and that is certainly how he came across then – and, for that matter, for the rest of his career.

George recalls meeting Graham Williams at a function a few years after the Albion full back had retired. Graham said to him that he wanted to look at him face-to-face, 'Because, he said, all he had ever seen of me was my backside and the number on my shirt. Not a hundred per cent true, but a nice compliment from a likeable and talented fellow pro.'

Even though he had done quite well, Busby, never one to rush a young player, pulled him out to make way for the return of Ian Moir followed by a switch to his place at outside right for David Herd. George returned to the Central League reserves and was given permission to go home to Belfast to be with his family over Christmas. There was a dramatic change of plan, though, after United crashed to a humiliating 6-1 defeat against Burnley at Turf Moor on Boxing Day 1963. With a return against Burnley just two days later, and, given the rivalry between the two clubs – after some steamy post-Munich matches enlivened by Burnley chairman Bob Lord describing United as 'playing like Teddy Boys' – there was a rapid change of plan. A telegram was sent to the Best home in Belfast instructing him to return to Old Trafford immediately.

George thought he was needed for the reserves, perhaps because of injuries, but his father reckoned a telegram signified something much more serious, like selection for the first team. They had a bet on it and his father won. Busby had dropped his two wingers, Shay Brennan and Albert Quixall, in favour of Willie Anderson and George Best.

United got their revenge with a 5-1 win that included a first League goal for Best, with Herd scoring twice and a further two from Graham Moore. George and Anderson rightly held their places for the following match, a third-round FA Cup tie against Southampton at The Dell. I recall interviewing George on the morning of the match because, as the FA Cup holders, United had become a focus for television and the press. I asked him if he was nervous or excited by all the fuss for one so young.

'No,' he replied, shrugging his shoulders to indicate what a daft question that was. He was sure of his talent and, to him, it was just another game of football. That ice in his veins, the cool dude approach, always marked him out before matches. He often stood outside the players' entrance chatting to friends until half an hour before kick-off. Meanwhile his team mates would be going through their various pre-match rituals and endeavouring to keep their tension under control.

United won that Cup tie with a performance from Best that clinched his place in the team until the end of the season. He made a total of 17 League appearances and scored three goals.

He also made his mark in the FA Cup, with seven appearances and two goals to help the Reds reach the semi-finals.

George was of course still young enough to play in the youth team and, though he missed the early rounds because of his first-team commitments, he was brought in for the final of the FA Youth Cup. He played in both legs against Swindon Town to win 5-2 on aggregate and claim the Cup for the 1963–64 season. Best scored in the first leg, a 1-1 draw at Swindon, and then watched his old house-mate David Sadler grab a brilliant hat-trick which, with a goal from John Aston, gave United a 4-1 win on the night and their first success in the youth competition since the Munich air crash. United had won the FA Youth Cup for five successive seasons from its inception in 1952, and this was a long-awaited return to those halcyon days and a further indication that Busby's years of rebuilding were beginning to bear fruit.

Sir Alex Ferguson's class of '92 that won the FA Youth Cup was rightly hailed as a vintage one, with players like David Beckham, Ryan Giggs, Gary Neville and Paul Scholes, who went on to form the backbone of both the United and England teams.

And the intake of young players in the Best era was an important stepping-stone along the way to complete recovery from the Munich calamity. Six players made it through to the first-team squad: George Best, David Sadler, John Aston, John Fitzpatrick, Jimmy Rimmer and Bobby Noble all went on to play senior football at Old Trafford with two more, Willie Anderson and Albert Kinsey, also playing for the first team before going on to successful careers with other clubs.

The jewel in the crown of this sparkling surge of youth, though, was undoubtedly George Best. The personal triumphs that played such a big part in creating one of Manchester United's most successful eras were about to come, not only for United, but at international level. George was capped for Northern Ireland after only 21 first-team games.

## 'EL BEATLE' ARRIVES

George Best grew quickly in stature and contributed hugely to Manchester United winning the championship in the 1964–65 season, their first League success in the rebuilding process after losing so many of their young stars in the Munich air crash of 1958. It was his first full season but what an impact he made. He missed only one League game and scored 10 goals in an all-action forward line.

The attack crackled with talent. Denis Law was at his peak, scoring 28 goals in 36 appearances. David Herd claimed his usual 20 which, with 15 from John Connelly and 10 from Bobby Charlton along with George's 10, saw them beat Leeds to the title on goal average. A 3-1 win against Leeds gave them the championship and it was the boy from Belfast who gave United the lead. He became the symbol of the new wave carrying the torch forward into a new era.

Most people agreed that United were now the best footballing side in the country and that in George Best they were rapidly developing one of the most exciting talents in the game. The championship put United back into Europe and gave George the opportunity to emerge as a superstar. The scene was set when United beat Benfica 3-2 in the first leg of the European Cup quarter final at Old Trafford. As Geoffrey Green, the distinguished football writer of *The Times* put it: 'One goal in the bank may not be enough for Manchester United. But at least this night cannot be taken away. It was something to remember.' But he could not have got it more wrong. Manchester United won the second leg 5-1 in Lisbon, standing normal football logic on its head. The most optimistic United supporter could not have foreseen such a dazzling display against the mighty Eagles, who had a fine record of 19 unbeaten European games on their own ground.

On this night, Wednesday 9 March 1966, Benfica were not just beaten, they were pulverised. All expectations and sense of planning indicated that United would open cautiously in an effort to safeguard their slim lead, but they were three up on the night after just 14 minutes. George Best, the 19-year-old Belfast genius touching new heights in his already meteoric career, scored the first two in the sixth and 12th minutes, and then two minutes later sent John Connelly in to slot home the third. There were 80,000 people crammed into the Estádio da Luz, most of them expecting to hail a Benfica triumph. And why shouldn't they have anticipated victory after winning 18 and drawing one of their European contests, scoring 78 goals in the process and conceding only 14? Never before had a visiting foreign side scored more than two goals in a match. The mood of the home crowd was one of noisy confidence and, as the 10pm kick-off approached, rockets shot into the night sky to celebrate the presentation of a statuette to Eusébio to mark his selection as European Footballer of the Year.

Within 12 minutes he should have handed over his award to the brilliant Best, the boy with the Beatle haircut who had produced such shimmering skills and spectacular craft to plunge the Stadium of Light into gloom. He scored his first goal with a header, leaving goalkeeper Costa Pereira stranded, from Tony Dunne's pinpoint free kick. His second followed a huge goal kick from Harry Gregg which Herd headed back and down into the path of the Irish youngster. Best streaked away past three white-shirted Benfica players as if they were statues before slamming a swift right foot shot low into the corner of the goal. Even now, looking back at old video footage of that goal, his speed and agility is breathtaking.

Law masterminded the third as he worked the ball in from a deep position to draw two defenders before slipping a pass to Best, who promptly played it further across to present John Connelly with a goal. United even had two efforts which found the net disallowed, so dominant were they in the first half. Early in the second Benfica got a goal back, but only with the help of Shay Brennan slicing the ball into his own net as he tried to clear, and even then it failed to fire the Portuguese into anything like their normally incisive form. It was as though they were still confounded by the visitors' opening onslaught.

Law laid on a fourth goal by finding an unmarked Pat Crerand on the penalty spot and near the end Charlton sailed through for a fine fifth goal to avenge the five-goal drubbing they had received in Lisbon just two years previously in the European Cup Winners' Cup. Revenge was now complete.

Back home, England prepared to hail a new hero now known as 'El Beatle', the accolade bestowed on the player by the press, who saw Best as English football's answer to the music of the Beatles. He was a stripling playing in only his third season of League football, but it was a defining moment – the emergence of a cult figure from football to represent the Swinging Sixties.

It was also the night which confirmed the birth of a new superstar as the player carried his domestic achievements on to a European stage. As for team tactics, Matt Busby laughed afterwards and said: 'I couldn't believe it. Out this kid comes as if he's never heard of tradition and starts running at them, turning them inside out. I ought to have shouted at him for not following instructions. But what can you say? He was a law unto himself. He always was. I was cross with him … almost!' George himself described the match in one of his books:

I felt superb. The atmosphere sent the blood coursing through my veins, adding power to my muscles, imagination to my brain. Why I played the way I did that night is one of those inexplicable things. Genius, and I believe on the football field I had it, something you simply can't begin to explain. I've been interviewed by American journalists to whom analysis is of the greatest importance. Why do you do this, and how? It all seems so important to them, whereas to me it's natural. Football is a simple game.

Perhaps in Lisbon I fell in love with the place where we stayed: Estoril. Sunny, beautiful sandy beach, lovely park, luxurious hotels. I just felt good all the time we were there. Even the jeering Benfica fans before the game didn't upset me, holding up five fingers to the coach windows as a sardonic reminder of our 5-0 defeat by Sporting Lisbon two years earlier in the Cup Winners' Cup quarter-final. We gave them five goals all right: and we put a stop to their damn firecrackers and rockets. They had been masters of Europe but we showed them how to play the game.

There was no doubt that George had instinctive flair off the field as well as on it. Hunting for souvenirs the morning after the match in Estoril he bought himself a huge floppy sombrero. He carried it through all the airport formalities and stuck with it on the journey home. Then, as the team walked off the plane in Manchester, he put the hat on his head. The press photographers were already looking for the game's scoring hero and now they were being presented with a publicity dream, an unusual and distinctive picture opportunity which duly hit the next day's papers. The *Daily Mirror* had him on both the front and back pages. George later admitted that later that month he had been due to open a boutique in Sale and he thought the sombrero would be a useful prop. He was right ... the picture went round the world and he was forever tagged 'El Beatle'.

The team that startled Europe in Lisbon was: Gregg, Brennan, Dunne, Crerand, Foulkes, Stiles, Best, Law, Charlton, Herd and Connelly. United were favourites to go all the way to at least the final, but they lost to Partizan Belgrade in the semi-finals. Significantly, Best was carrying an injury in the first leg and was out of the second having a cartilage operation. It seemed that when George went, the magic went as well.

The older players knew time was running out for them and Pat Crerand vowed to Busby that they would win the Championship the following season to give the maestro one final bid for European glory. It turned out to be no empty promise as United finished the season with a flourish, beating West Ham in London 6-1 to take the title by four points from Nottingham Forest. Best played throughout the season and scored his usual 10 goals to help give the old men of the team their final chance to conquer Europe.

## BORN TO PLAY

The season Manchester United won the European Cup was George's best ever. In the League he scored 28 goals in 41 appearances, overshadowing Denis Law for the first time. It was the changing of the guard. The Irishman was just as important on the road to the 1968 final against Benfica at Wembley. He was quiet in the early rounds but came to the fore in the semi-final against Real Madrid, when he scored in the 1-0 win in the opening leg at Old Trafford. In Spain the Reds were facing defeat 3-2 until George sensed the moment to strike with a piercing run down the right wing to roll the ball across for Bill Foulkes, who had left his defensive lines, to score. It was the equaliser in the 3-3 draw but of course United won on aggregate. The European Cup was finally won as much by character as ability. Matt Busby described it as 'heart', the kind of fighting spirit that his team had shown to pull the game out of the fire in Madrid.

It was harder going against the Portuguese champions with tension seeming to cramp the style of both teams. Perhaps because the match was being played on home soil, United were the first to settle and soon began taking the game to their opponents.

Crucial duels were taking place all over the field. Bill Foulkes knew he had to win the aerial battle with the towering Torres, and Nobby Stiles was certainly aware that his marking of the elusive Eusébio was critical. Benfica also knew they had particular players to mark and the rugged Cruz became George Best's watchdog, several times bringing him down without hesitation. When Cruz missed him on one occasion Humberto sailed in and was booked.

United's persistence in attack took a long time to find a chink in the visitors' defence, until in the 53rd minute David Sadler crossed from a deep position on the left for Bobby Charlton to jump and glance the ball over the goalkeeper into the far corner of the net. That was the signal for Benfica to throw caution to the wind and step up their own forward momentum, drawing on the experience garnered from playing in five European Cup finals. Nine minutes from the end they pulled level through a finely worked goal. Augusto put the ball in for Torres to nod down. Eusébio made a run which drew the defence, and it was Jaime Graça who latched on to the ball to score with a fierce shot from a narrow angle.

This was the moment when United needed all the heart they could muster. Benfica stepped up the pressure and twice Eusébio broke through to test Alex Stepney. His last effort brought him face-to-face with the United goalkeeper and he unleashed a rocket that Stepney saved with such effect that even his opponent applauded!

United were faltering and as Stiles put it later: 'If the game had had another 10 minutes without a break I think we would have lost.'

Extra time opened dramatically as United played with renewed heart to sweep forward and score twice in two minutes. In only the third minute Brian Kidd headed on Alex Stepney's clearance to Best who immediately headed for goal. He took the ball round the defenders in a curving arc and then past the goalkeeper before popping it into an empty net. It was George at his very best and Kidd was quick to match him with a goal to mark his 19th birthday. Kidd whipped in a close range header that was blocked by Henrique but as the ball came back the youngster got in a second header that this time looped over the goalkeeper. Kidd then laid on a goal for Bobby Charlton and United triumphed with a 4-1 victory. Denis Law, recovering from a knee operation, had watched the game from his hospital bed in Manchester. He had had a frustrating season but his place had been more than adequately filled by a dynamic Best.

The teams in the European Cup final at Wembley on 29 May 1968, with United wearing a deep blue strip, were:

Manchester United: Stepney, Brennan, Dunne, Crerand, Foulkes, Stiles, Best, Kidd, Charlton, Sadler, Aston. Sub: Rimmer.

Benfica: Henrique, Adolfo, Humberto, Jacinto, Cruz, Graça, Coluna, Augusto, Torres, Eusébio, Simões. Sub: Nasimento.

It was the crowning moment for George Best, the pinnacle of his young career. Before long fame and fortune would start eating away at his football. Once a match or training session was over

George became more and more distant from his team-mates. The older ones were married, mostly with young families. They went home, leaving George to amuse himself. The bright lights began to beckon with the clubs and the girls beginning to loom large in his life. His friend and one-time fellow lodger David Sadler, who knew him well, in good times and bad, summed up George's career to me:

There was nothing complicated about George, certainly not in the early years. All he wanted to do was to play football. He and I were very much of an age, although by the time I arrived he had been to Manchester, returned homesick to Ireland and then come back to Old Trafford. We signed as professionals at about the same time and became pals, eventually sharing digs for about six years and rooming together when we travelled.

We were both part of a successful United youth team, and in 1964 we won the club's first FA Youth Cup since pre-Munich days. Although I made my senior debut ahead of George, I was in and out for some years, but once George stepped up he was on an escalator to the skies.

The minute you started playing with him, even in a kick-around, it was blatantly obvious to everybody that he was special, and nothing was ever a surprise afterwards. He was born to play football.

Nominally he was a winger, but he enjoyed a free role and just played the game. He was never restricted to supplying crosses or hogging the touchline – that would have been foolish. My main thought when playing was 'Let's get the bloody ball to him as quickly as we can, because that's the most likely way that we're going to earn a bonus!'

George's greatest strength was that he didn't have a weakness. Bobby Charlton, for instance, was a great player but not a good tackler. George was. In fact, there was a time when he could have played anywhere in the team and been the best in that position. It sounds incredible, but by the middle to late 1960s he could do everything better than everybody else.

He could tackle and defend as well as anyone; he was instinctive but understood the technical aspects of the game; he could shoot and beat people, and he knew when to pass (usually!). True, some people thought he was greedy on occasions, but as he matured everything fell into place.

When you make your debut, the best you can hope is that you fit in and do your bit, that you don't let the team down. George did that from the word go. There was never the slightest doubt that he was worth his place. By the early 1970s, under Frank O'Farrell, he was carrying the team, all the way to the top of the league for a while. With the team falling apart, he became the team, and it must have been frustrating for him.

Much is written about the waste of George not playing on until he was 36, but I never think about that. I just think of the brilliant work that he did, what he gave to United and the game.

It is easy to analyse his career from this distance, but back then it wasn't. He became the first pop-star footballer, and nobody could have known how to react to all that entailed. Even Matt Busby, with all his wisdom and under-standing of people, could only relate George to situations he had dealt with earlier. But here was someone totally different.

The triumph at Wembley in 1968 was the culmination of Manchester United's European crusade, but also it was the end of something, certainly for Matt, who had never been really fit after Munich. But George was only 22 and understandably he felt it should have signalled the lift-off to even greater achievements. Even Matt, for once in his life, had not looked beyond his current team. Pre-Munich he was building for the future, after Munich he was rebuild-ing out of pure necessity, with no thought of what should follow in the 1970s and 1980s, and the club suffered for that.

Other top players might have gained consolation from international foot-ball, but George knew he was unlikely to feature in any World Cup Finals, and I believe that became a major factor in the frustration which contributed to his subsequent problems.

But whatever is said about George Best, I am certain of one thing – he was the greatest footballer I ever played with or against.

## TROUBLED TIMES

Inevitably, and rightly so, the accolades poured in: George was chosen as Northern Ireland's Player of the Year, the Football Writers' Association voted him Footballer of the Year and six months later he joined an elite band as European Footballer of the Year, the youngest ever. The following season, 1968–69, saw him once more in dominant form with 19 goals in 41 appearances helping United, defending their title, to the semi-finals of the European Cup.

Cracks were beginning to appear, though, and in the First Division United slipped to a finishing place of 11th. The club was heading for a period of change and troubled times were ahead for both Manchester United and George Best. Sir Matt Busby, who appeared to have lost his toughness and was too kind-hearted to break up the team that had brought him his European triumph, retired. Reserve team coach Wilf McGuinness, who had served the club in various capacities for over 17 years (he was one of the original 'Busby Babes' before his playing career was cut short through injury) lasted as manager for 18 months, from mid-1969 to the end of 1970. Sir Matt Busby returned as stop-gap manager and in 1971 former Irish International Frank O'Farrell was appointed from Leicester City. After a disastrous year in 1972 he was also summarily removed. The last thing George needed was this kind of rudderless management. From being a hero he became a headache.

The 1969–70 season saw him sent off on a number of occasions, the first time for knocking the ball out of referee Jack Taylor's hands, the second time playing for Ireland, when he was reported for throwing mud and spitting at referee Eric Jennings. He served a month's suspension for the first offence but amid much acrimony escaped punishment for the second with the support of the Northern Irish FA who wanted him available for the next international.

Despite these setbacks he still managed to score 15 goals to help United finish eighth in the League, and scored 18 goals in each of his next two seasons, missing only four games. In February 1970 he scored six of United's eight goals in an 8-2 win against Northampton Town, and in 1971 twice scored hat-tricks. He was doing more than his fair share, but increasingly he felt that the club was going nowhere and that he was being asked to carry his fading team-mates. Still in his early twenties, the pressure to perform, the disruption at United and the constant media attention were beginning to take their toll. His motivation was low and he began drinking too much and having black-outs.

Behind the scenes he was becoming increasingly difficult to manage. He failed to turn up for training on Christmas Day 1970. Earlier, Wilf McGuinness had found himself in a real dilemma when he caught George with a girl in his room a couple of hours before an FA Cup semi-final against Leeds. The situation called for disciplinary action but how can you drop your best player? Wilf played him but his behaviour was dividing the dressing-room. A month later in January 1971 he failed to turn up for the match against Chelsea, staying with the Irish actress Sinead Cusack instead. The media scrum that ensued went on for four days, with the beleaguered George besieged in Sinead's north London flat. Later that year, before the Newcastle match in October, the IRA threatened to shoot him. It was not a good year for George Best. Wilf McGuinness's successor Frank O'Farrell once told me that he would never do any good at Old Trafford until the European stars had gone, but he needed time for that which in the end he didn't have.

The year 1972 was the beginning of the end when in January George walked out and missed a week's training. United ordered him to move back into digs with Mrs Fullaway instead of living on his own – except for girlfriends – in the house he had had built for himself in Cheshire's leafy Bramhall. That didn't work and at the end of the season he skipped United's trip to Israel and turned up instead on the Costa del Sol, from where with the help of an avid media he held press conferences claiming he was drinking a bottle of vodka a day. 'Mentally I am a bloody wreck, and I'm finished with football,' he declared. In May, at the age of 26, he had announced his retirement. But he changed his mind, came back and was given two weeks' suspension by O'Farrell, who also told him to go and live with Pat Crerand and his family in an effort to get some order back into his life. That didn't last very long either. 'I think my kids drove him mad,' said Pat. The autumn of 1972 was not a good time for United or Best. Results were bad and George's behaviour increasingly erratic. In early December United put Best up for transfer (the letter to him crossing with one from George once more announcing his retirement) and just before Christmas sacked Frank O'Farrell after a 0-5 drubbing by Crystal Palace, appointing Crerand and Bill Foulkes as caretaker managers.

In December 1972 Tommy Docherty inherited the problem and persevered with patience. Once he had actually got George out on to the training pitch or in a game he was no problem. Following a thrombosis in his leg that summer, from which he could potentially have died, George also felt that he had been spared and determined to get fit once more. George still had his love for football; it was the bits in between that had become the problem. He played fitfully throughout

1973, playing his last game for United on 1 January 1974, losing 0-3 to Queen's Park Rangers. Finally, after missing training the following week, he was dropped. He never played for United again.

It was a sad end. He later played for Hibernian, Dunstable, Stockport County, Fulham and in America where he enjoyed a new lease of life in the slower-paced game played in the United States.

George felt many of his and United's problems stemmed from winning the European Cup. 'It was as if everyone thought that winning the European Cup was the ultimate achievement. They were happy to relax and rest on their laurels. But to me, with a whole career ahead of me, it looked as if the future contained nothing but grafting about in the middle of the table, losing as many games as we won.'

That could well be half the story but, as we know more clearly now, the demon drink was also taking its grip. His team-mates were divided in their views. One player who only caught the tail end of his career at Old Trafford said: 'George thought he was the James Bond of soccer. He had everything he wanted and he pleased himself. He had money, girls and tremendous publicity. He lived from day to day and right to the end he got away with it when he missed training or ran away. So he didn't care. People made excuses for him. He didn't even have to bother to make them for himself. People talk about pressures and depressions. It was rubbish. He just didn't have any responsibilities, nothing to worry about at all. All kinds of people covered up for him, even the press, and he was lucky to get away with it for so long.'

A harsh judgement. Most of his peers were simply lost in admiration for his talent. As Harry Gregg puts it: 'From the first time I met him in 1962 until I left in '67, he was always a pleasant, well-mannered young man. Whatever his problems were off the field, on it "the little fellah", as Matt Busby and I called him, could be sublime. When George was on song, he was blessed with greatness. He was ice cold, and seemingly free from nerves, even on the big occasions. He had no fear, he could tackle as well as take people on, he was good in the air and there was a devilment about his play when required. Above all, he was supremely confident. George produced some stunning performances'.

Sir Bobby Charlton admired him, though he did get frustrated by him when they played together. He tells the story of how he used to wait for passes that never came and that George would use him as a dummy only to stay on a run with the ball. He did that in one match to leave Bobby starting to call him a greedy so-and-so only to find himself exploding: 'What a great goal.'

Denis Law says he loved playing with George and that 'without doubt he was the most gifted player I played with or against. He had buckets of talent and — it may surprise some to hear this — he was also one of the best, most dedicated trainers I came across. Although he looked to be all skin and bone he was built like a whippet.'

Alex Stepney believes it was his great fitness that enabled the player to carry on playing to such a high standard even after he had launched himself down the slippery slope of late nights and drinking too much.

As Nobby Stiles says in his book: 'George was a skinny kid when he arrived at Old Trafford and he never got to have much flesh on him. The strength sprang from deep inside him. He was a phenomenal trainer, and that was true whatever the situation. He could arrive unshaved and smelling of booze, but he was still brilliant when the work started. He was a lovely lad, too, there was no edge to him.'

## Career Record Excluding NASL

### Manchester United
5/63 – 1/74
Total appearances: 466, Total goals: 178
League appearances: 361, Goals: 137
FA Cup appearances: 46, Goals: 21
League Cup appearances: 25, Goals 9
European appearances: 34, Goals 11

### Jewish Guild
5/74 – 6/74
League appearances: 5, Goals: n/k

### Stockport County
11/75 – 12/75
League appearances: 3, Goals: 2

### Cork Celtic
12/75 – 1/76
League appearances: 3, Goals: 2

### Fulham
9/76 – 5/77; 9/77 – 11/77
Total appearances: 47, Total goals: 12
League appearances: 42, Goals: 8
FA Cup appearances: 2, Goals: 2
League Cup appearances: 3, Goals: 2

### Hibernian
11/79 – 4/80; 9/80 – 10/80
Total appearances: 22, Total goals: 3
League appearances: 17, Goals: 3
FA Cup appearances: 3, Goals: 0
League Cup appearances: 2, Goals: 0

### AFC Bournemouth
3/83 – 5/83
League appearances: 5, Goals: 0

### Brisbane Lions
7/83
League appearances: 4, Goals: 0

**Total games played: 584, Total goals: 193**

## Career Record in NASL

### Los Angeles Aztecs
4/76 – 8/76; 5/77 – 8/77; 4/78 – 6/78
Total appearances: 61, Total goals: 29
Regular season appearances: 55, Goals: 27
Play off appearances: 6, Goals: 2

### Fort Lauderdale Strikers
6/78 – 8/78; 3/79 – 7/79
Total apperances: 33, Goals: 7
Regular season appearances: 28, Goals: 6
Play off appearances: 5, Goals: 1

### San Jose Earthquakes
4/80 – 8/80; 3/81 – 8/81
Regular season appearances: 56, Goals: 21

**Total games played: 150, Total goals: 57**

Early Years

'I think I've found a genius.'

**Bob Bishop, Manchester United scout, 1961**

**Above**  A seven-year-old George poses with Carol, the oldest of his three sisters, in 1953.

**Left**  The beginning of a promising career… the young Manchester United winger.

**Above** A seventeen-year-old Best signs autographs for eager young fans after United's 1-0 win against Aston Villa in April 1964.

**Left** Best scores his first League goal in a 5-1 win against Burnley in December 1963, in only his second league appearance for United.

'George had this wondrous ability which set him apart from virtually everyone else who has ever played the game.'
**Paddy Crerand**

**Left** Making adjustments to his hairstyle in the dressing-room mirror. He was always immaculately turned out after matches.

**Right** More hair-grooming after training at The Cliff.

**Previous** Bobby Keetch of Fulham slides to block a shot during the match at Craven Cottage in March 1964. Best shows his innate sense of balance, always one of his most valuable attributes.

'It was a simple team talk. All I used to say was: "Whenever possible give the ball to George".'
**Sir Matt Busby**

**Above** Warming up for a match
at Old Trafford in December 1964.

**Right** George shows off his
skills to a fan.

**Above** George stands outside the doorway of 9 Aycliffe Avenue, Chorlton-cum-Hardy in Manchester, the house where he lodged with landlady Mrs Mary Fullaway after joining United as a youngster. The suit, tie and winkle-picker shoes were all the rage.

**Left** Best in action in March 1969.

**Overleaf** Best relaxes at Mrs Fullaway's, playing music on his 'radiogram' in September 1964.

'George had more ways of beating a player than anyone I've ever seen. He was unique in his gifts.'
**Sir Matt Busby**

**Previous**  Always a natty dresser…

**Above**  At home against Blackburn
Rovers in November 1965. Best
dances past goalkeeper Fred Else
to score in a 2-2 draw.

**Overleaf** George in full flight, perfectly in control of the ball, during a league match in January 1966.

'He has ice in his veins, warmth in his heart and timing and balance in his feet.'
**Danny Blanchflower, former Northern Ireland captain, 1970**

'From 1964 to 1969 he was the best player in the country. I'd put him on a par with the top six players I ever saw. Bestie belongs among the elite.'
**Denis Law**

**Left** Wearing the souvenir sombrero on his return to Manchester Airport following United's defeat of Benfica 5-1 in the second leg of the European Cup quarter-final. George scored United's first two goals and the press were waiting for him – this iconic photograph was used all around the world.

**Right** Bobby Charlton, Denis Law, George Best and Bill Foulkes celebrating after winning the League Championship in May 1967.

**Previous** (Left) Wolves go into a two-goal lead with penalties in the FA Cup quarter-final. This is the moment George Best gave United the lead for the first time in the match, only 18 minutes from the end. United went on to win 4-2. (Right) George airborne in the European Cup semi-final against Partizan Belgrade. United lost the away game 2-0, and won the home game 1-0 at Old Trafford, to make an unexpected exit from the competition.

**Overleaf** Beating (left to right) Paddy Crerand, Frank McLintock and John Radford to the ball in this match against Arsenal in 1967.

'He belongs to the list of greats with Charlton, Dalglish, Finney and Shackleton – and right at the top.'
**Sir Bobby Robson**

'He was the greatest British player of all time.'
**Tommy Docherty, Manchester United manager December 1972 – July 1977**

**Left** George turns to celebrate his goal against Benfica in the first minute of extra time in the European Cup Final at Wembley Stadium in May 1968. United went on to win 4-1.

**Above** The winning team: (back row) Bill Foulkes, John Aston, Jimmy Rimmer, Alex Stepney, Alan Gowling, David Herd; (middle) David Sadler, Tony Dunne, Shay Brennan, Pat Crerand, George Best, Francis Burns, Jack Crompton (trainer); (front) Jimmy Ryan, Nobby Stiles, Denis Law, Matt Busby (manager), Bobby Charlton, Brian Kidd, John Fitzpatrick.

**Left** Celebrating Bobby Charlton's goal in the victory over Benfica.

**Above** Ron Harris keeps an eye on George as he leaps for a header in a 2-0 win against Chelsea in 1968, rated by many as one of Best's finest League performances.

**Right** In a later match against Chelsea, in 1971, George skilfully survives a tackle by Ron 'Chopper' Harris.

'It seems impossible to hurt him. All manner of men have tried to intimidate him. Best merely glides along, riding tackles and brushing giants aside like leaves.'
**Joe Mercer, Manchester City manager, 1969**

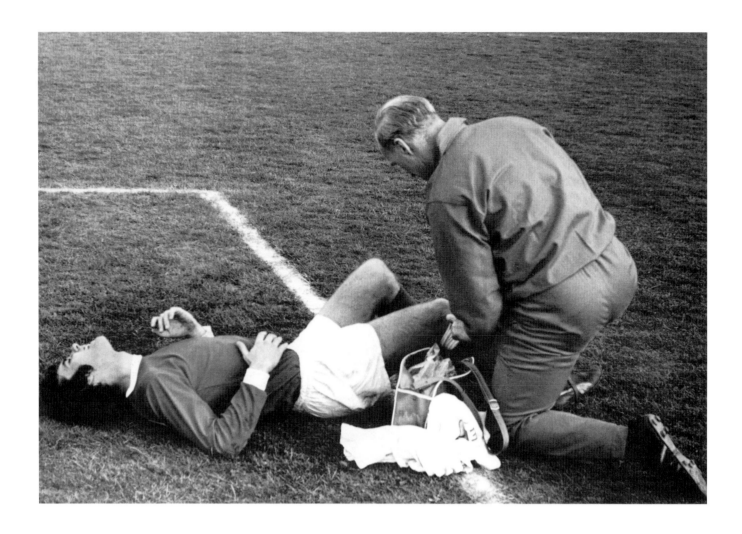

'We had our problems with the wee fella,
but I prefer to remember his genius.'
**Sir Matt Busby, 1988**

**Above**  It's not all wine and
roses… trouble with the right
knee in 1966, treated here by
trainer Jack Crompton, an injury
that finally landed him in hospital
for a cartilage operation.

**Right**  Often the most skilled
player on the pitch, Best was
made the target of the
opposition's hardmen. Best
reacts, and has to be held
back by United's own enforcer,
Nobby Stiles.

**Left** Best was a great all-round player. Highly skilful, tough in the tackle and a master of the air…

**Above** Man of the moment: a celebrity on and off the pitch.

**Left** (Top) Opening his trendy boutique in Cross Street, Sale, and signing autographs for adoring young fans in March 1966. (Bottom) Getting to grips with his female customers' vital statistics, December 1966.

**Above** The Best of times…

Manchester United 1970–1973

**Left** George Best caught on camera before a fifth-round FA Cup tie against Northampton Town in February 1970.

**Above** Best glances back whilst offering a comforting arm to his United team-mate Bobby Charlton.

**Overleaf** George takes on the Leeds United defence. Such are his skills Best is watched closely by Billy Bremner, Norman Hunter and Terry Cooper.

'Unquestionably the greatest. There was simply nobody to compare with him.'
**Sir Alex Ferguson**

**Above** Best transfixes the crowd with his poise and balance in this FA Cup tie against Northampton Town. Best goes on to score six, a club record for the most goals in a single match. United won the game 8-2.

**Above** A man of fashion
standing outside his Bridge
Street boutique, Edwardia,
in Manchester.

**Overleaf** Best reels away in
celebration after scoring the first
of his six goals in the fifth round of
the FA Cup against Northampton
Town in February 1970.

'The closest I got to him was when we shook hands at the end of the game.'
**Roy Fairfax, Northampton Town, who had been marking Best when he scored six goals in the 8-2 FA Cup win for Manchester Utd, 1970**

'We hadn't a chance against United with Best in that form. Not even the Berlin Wall could have stopped him.'
**Kim Book, goalkeeper for Northampton Town, beaten a record six times by Best during the 8-2 victory in the 1970 FA Cup Final**

**Left** Getting ready to make the next move…

**Left** George's mesmerising ball skills and powerful runs made him a threat to any defence.

**Above** Best attempts an acrobatic shot at goal as the defender hopelessly looks on.

**Previous** Leeds United defender
Paul Reaney desperately pursues
Best.

**Left** The classic pre-season pose
at a photo session at Old Trafford.

**Above** With Denis Law, two
masters at unlocking defences
celebrating another breakthrough.

'He had stardust on him, absolute stardust. He elevated the
game in this country and we players ... all hoped some of that
stardust would fall on us as well.'
**Bob Wilson, former Arsenal goalkeeper**

**Previous** George and Crystal Palace's John Sewell battle shoulder to shoulder to reach a through-ball.

**Left** As much a fashion icon as a footballer, he was increasingly in demand off the pitch.

**Above** Football's first celebrity superstar, always the centre of attention, can be seen here in the company of Radio One DJ Dave Lee Travis and nightclub owner Willie Morgan.

'George should be remembered as the very best at what he did.
He was quite simply a football genius.'

**Bertie Ahern**

**Above**  George fires a shot at goal to score and complete his hat-trick against West Ham United in September 1971.

**Above left**  Best shows his skills in the FA Cup with Norman Hunter in hot pursuit while fellow Leeds United hardman Billy Bremner looks on.

'George had this wondrous ability which set him apart from virtually everyone else who has ever played the game.'

**Paddy Crerand, Manchester United team-mate**

**Left** George Best, playing for Northern Ireland, runs at the England defence at Windsor Park in May 1971. Best famously kicked the ball out of England goalkeeper Gordon Banks's hands as he was about to kick it, and scored. The goal was disallowed but it was later argued that it should have stood. England won 1-0.

**Above** George takes time
away from football with his
actress girlfriend Susan George,
relaxing on the beach in Majorca.

**Above** Forever surrounded by fans, George leaves training in his E-type Jaguar. But his increasingly fast-paced lifestyle soon began to affect his game.

'No situation is bigger than him. He can rise to any level and with experience he will be a giant. When he learns to use his natural ability with complete discipline he will be the finished article… perfect.'
**Sir Matt Busby, 1968**

**Above and Right**  Arguably the most naturally gifted footballer the British Isles has ever produced demonstrates his eye for the ball.

**Above and Right** George
shows off his ball juggling skills.

Left (Top) Manchester United
manager Tommy Docherty
invites Best back to the fold
in September 1973.
(Bottom) Looking happy and well
turned out, George was in good
form when he recommenced
training with his old team.

Right After an 11-month lay-off,
Best returns to first team football
– but it didn't last long, before
he quit Old Trafford for good.

**Distant Outposts**

**Left** It's not the all-white strip of Real Madrid but that of non-league Dunstable Town. This unlikely alliance was a favour for George's old friend and the then Dunstable manager Barry Fry, who knew that Best's guest appearance in a pre-season friendly would draw in the crowds. In the summer of 1974 Best turned out for Dunstable against a Manchester United XI, ironically whilst still under contract to the Red Devils.

**Above** Fry's prediction proved correct as 10,000 turned up to watch Best in action and a further 5,000 were left disappointed outside the stadium.

'I'd give all the champagne I've ever drunk to be playing alongside him in a big European match at Old Trafford.'
**Eric Cantona**

Left The North American Soccer League was enjoying huge success in the latter half of the 1970s. With huge crowds it briefly challenged the dominant homegrown US sports. Best scored 57 goals in 150 appearances for the Los Angeles Aztecs, the Fort Lauderdale Strikers (pictured) and the San Jose Earthquakes.

Right Perhaps the two greatest players of all time? The game in the Yankee stadium on 17 May 1976 between the Los Angeles Aztecs and the New York Cosmos drew around 70,000. Though Best was never to play in a World Cup, his time in the NASL pitted him against many of world football's superstars including Pele.

'Pele called me the greatest footballer in the world.
That is the ultimate salute to my life.'
**George Best**

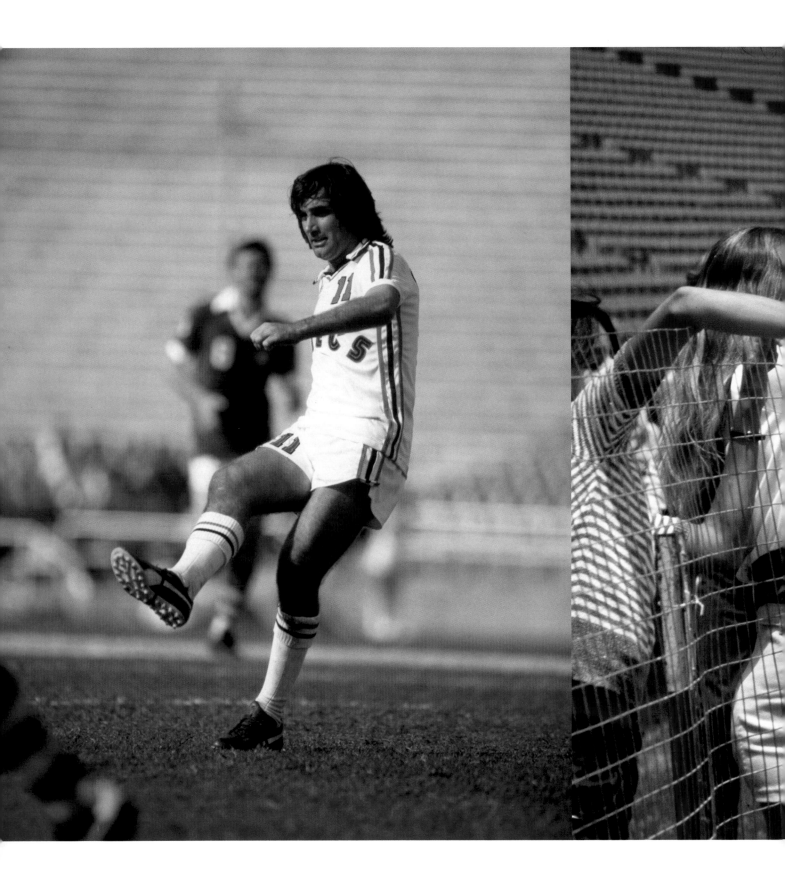

**Above** Training for the
Los Angeles Aztecs in 1978.

**Above** A Hollywood star?
George is welcomed by
adoring (and mostly female)
fans in Los Angeles.

**Left**  In his first game for Fulham at Craven Cottage, Best takes the ball past Alan Warboys of Bristol Rovers in typical fashion.

**Right**  (Top) The trio of Best, World Cup hero Bobby Moore and the young Rodney Marsh made Fulham the glamour club of West London in 1976. (Bottom) All eyes are on Best as he takes a corner for the Cottagers.

**Overleaf**  Having left the defender on the ground Best tests Blackburn Rovers goalkeeper Paul Bradshaw with a stinging shot on goal.

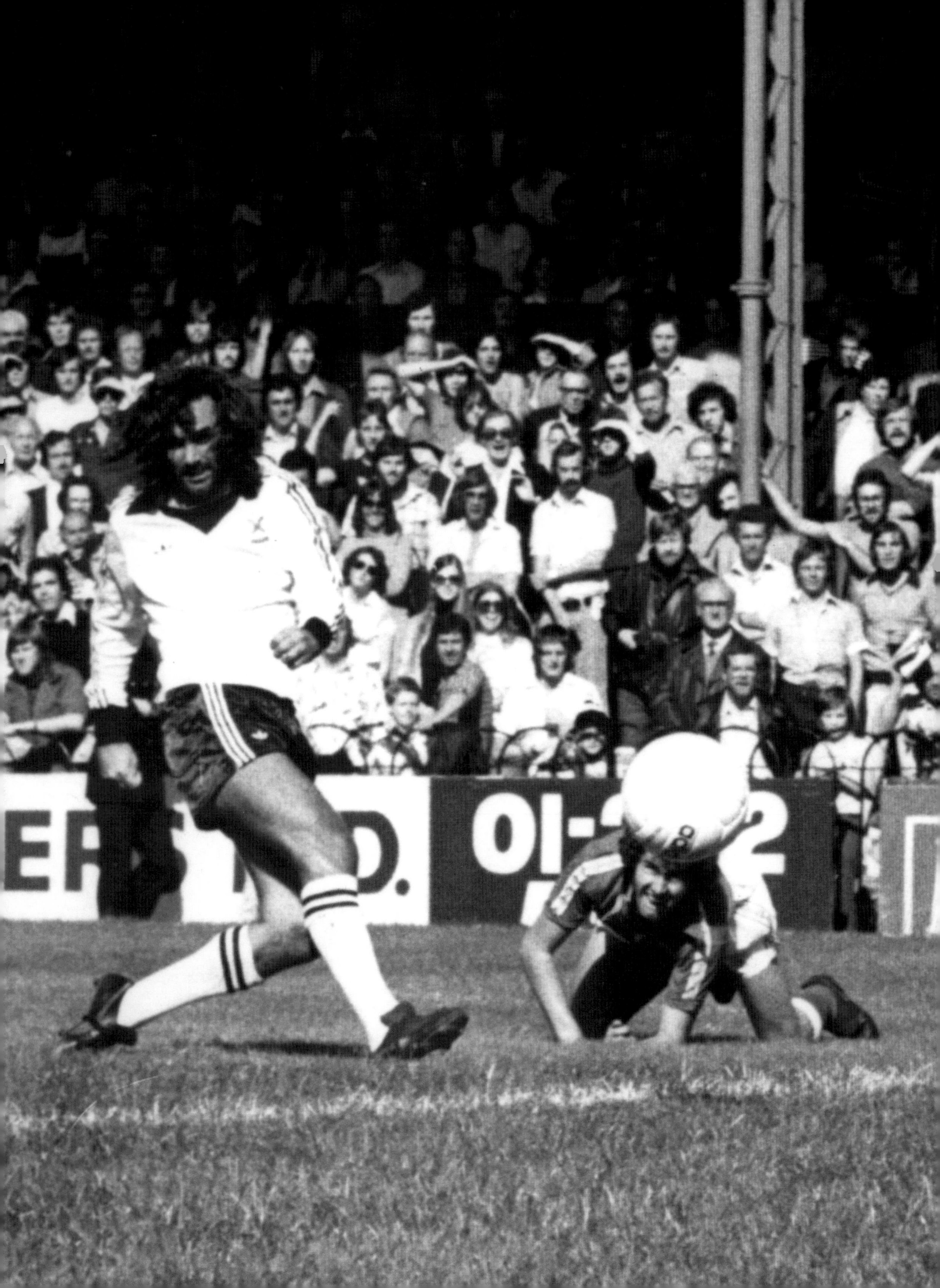
ER
D.
OI-
2

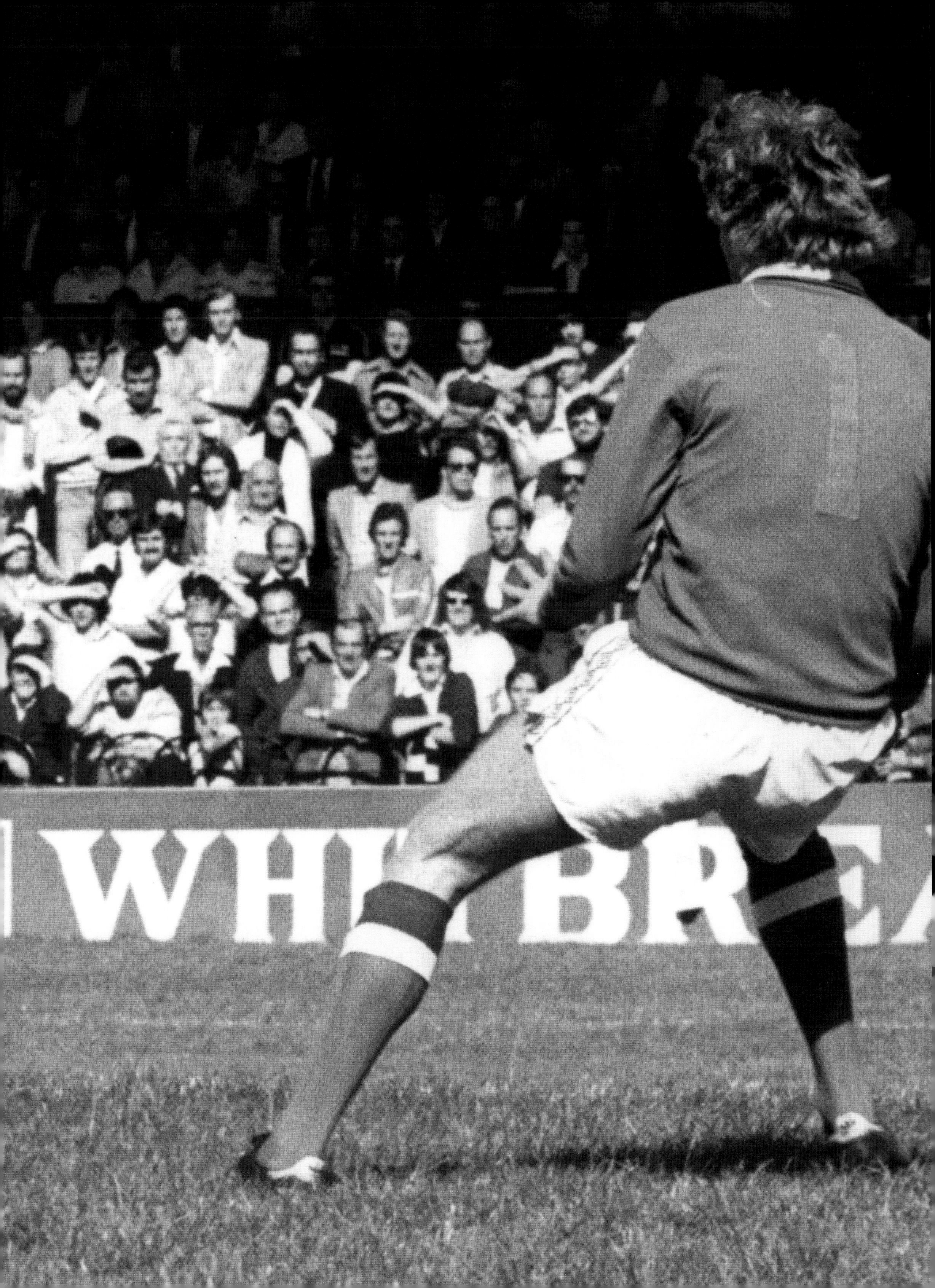

**Left** Playing for Hibernian in 1979.

**Right** Despite rumours that he was on the verge of being brought back to Old Trafford by Ron Atkinson as late as 1981, by March 1983 Best was lining up for Third Division strugglers AFC Bournemouth.

'He was able to use either foot – sometimes he seemed to have six.'
**Sir Matt Busby**

**Right** Wearing the colours of Manchester United,
Best enjoys a kickabout with local kids on a beach in
Mauritius only days after his release from Ford Open
Prison, where he had spent Christmas 1984 as part
of a three-month sentence for drink driving, assault
and failure to answer bail.

**GEORGE BEST**

1946 – 2005

**Above** A Belfast boy, wearing the Number 7 shirt Best made famous, pays tribute at a mural in Windsor Park, home of the Northern Irish national team.

'George inspired me when I was young. He was flamboyant and exciting and able to inspire his team-mates. We were very similar players, dribblers who were able to create moments of magic.'
**Diego Maradona**

'What he had was unique, you can't coach it. I think if you talk about the top European players, you talk about five or six and he will always be in there.'
**Johan Cruyff**

'George Best was spectacular, a genius.'
**Eusébio**

'Best was the greatest football player I ever saw.'
**Michael Parkinson**

**Above** A candle of remembrance in tribute to a footballing legend.

'Manchester United's glorious history has been created by people like Best. Anyone that witnessed what George could do on the pitch wished they could do the same. He made an immense contribution to the game and enriched the lives of everyone who saw him play. Football has lost one of its greats, and I've lost a dear friend.'
**Sir Bobby Charlton**

'He was a genius on the pitch, one of the finest players the world has ever seen.'
**Gordon Taylor, PFA chief executive**

'You will never have played with anybody like him and you never will again.'
**Sir Matt Busby**

'As a Manchester United fan, it was a proud moment for me when I wore the same Number 7 shirt as him. He was a football legend. He was one of the greatest players to have ever graced the game and a great person as well.'

**David Beckham**

'He was not only a fantastic player, to me he was also a fantastic bloke.'

**Former Northern Ireland team and room-mate Pat Jennings**

'Such men do not die, they live on. In ten years' time, my children will still be watching videos of George Best.'

**José Mourinho**

'George Best was the best player the UK has ever produced.'

**Sir Bobby Robson**

**Above** Banners displayed by fans of AS Roma at their Olympic stadium on 27th November 2005 reveal how George's skills are world-renowned. They read, 'Goodbye George, your soccer was the Best!'

'The most naturally gifted player I have ever seen.'
**Johnny Giles, Leeds United**

'One of the most charming fellows I ever met.'
**Terry Wogan**

'George Best was one of the greatest footballers of all time. Naturally athletic, tough, confident and blessed with genius, his career was one of the brightest stars of its generation. For all the goals, the audacious dribbles and all the wonderful memories, Manchester United and its legions of fans worldwide will always be grateful. We feel a deep sense of loss but his spirit and his talent will live on forever.'
**Manchester United official statement**

**Left** Mikael Silvestre, Paul Scholes, Ji-Sung Park, Wes Brown, Wayne Rooney and Alan Smith join in a spontaneous minute's applause in memory of George Best at West Ham United.

'I hope they remember the football.'
**George Best**

# Chronology

**1946**
22 MAY  George Best born in Belfast.

**1961**
16 AUGUST  Joins Manchester United as an amateur.

**1963**
22 MAY  Signs professional forms with Manchester United.
14 SEPTEMBER  League debut against West Bromwich
Albion at Old Trafford, aged 17. United win 1-0.
28 DECEMBER  Scores first league goal at home
against Burnley.

**1964**
15 APRIL  Makes Northern Ireland debut in 3-2 win
against Wales in Swansea.
30 SEPTEMBER  In a 2-0 away win against Chelsea,
Best is applauded off the pitch by 61,000 home supporters.
14 NOVEMBER  Scores first goal for Northern Ireland
in a 1-2 away defeat against Switzerland.

**1965**
Manchester United win their first League Championship
in eight years.

**1966**
9 MARCH  Scores twice in a 5-1 away win against Benfica
in the second leg of the European Cup quarter-final tie.
Best is launched as a superstar, earning the nickname
'El Beatle'.

**1967**
Manchester United win the League Championship.
21 OCTOBER  Plays in what many believe to be his finest
performance for his country in a home win for Northern
Ireland against Scotland.

**1968**
4 MAY  Voted British Footballer of the Year.
29 MAY  Scores in Manchester United's 4-1 victory
against Benfica in the final of the European Cup
at Wembley Stadium.
16 OCTOBER  Sent off for the first time in his playing
career against Estudiantes at Old Trafford.

**1969**
5 APRIL  Awarded European Footballer of the Year.

**1970**
7 FEBRURARY  Scores a double hat-trick against
Northampton in the fifth round of the FA Cup.
Manchester United win 8-2.
18 APRIL  Sent off playing for Northern Ireland against
Scotland in Belfast for throwing mud at referee.

**1971**
17 NOVEMBER  Best is subject of 'This Is Your Life'.

**1972**
20 MAY  Best announces that he is retiring from football
and is drinking a bottle of spirits a day.
7 JULY  Announces that he will again play for
Manchester United, but is suspended for two weeks
for a breach of contract.
19 DECEMBER  United manager Frank O'Farrell
is sacked. Best announces his retirement from football
for the second time.

**1973**
28 AUGUST  Makes short comeback after making peace
with new United boss Tommy Docherty.

**1974**
1 JANUARY  Best's final game for Manchester United
is a 0-3 defeat against Queens Park Rangers.
MAY  Plays briefly with the Jewish Guild in Johannesburg.

**1975**
8 NOVEMBER  Released from contract with
Manchester United.
10 NOVEMBER  Signs for one month to play home games
for Stockport County.
DECEMBER  Signs for Los Angeles Aztecs in the newly
formed North American Soccer League and plays briefly
with Cork Celtic.

**1976**
12 AUGUST  Signs a contract to play for Fulham.
13 OCTOBER  Makes 'comeback' appearance for
Northern Ireland against Holland.

**1977**
12 OCTOBER  Makes the last of 37 international
appearances for Northern Ireland against Holland in Belfast.
12 NOVEMBER  Plays his final game for Fulham against
Stoke City. Fulham lose 0-2.

**1978**

24 JANUARY Marries Angela MacDonald Janes, aged 25, in Las Vegas.
20 JUNE Plays his final game for Los Angeles Aztecs against the Washington Diplomats, losing 0-4.
JUNE Transferred to Fort Lauderdale Strikers. Receives a worldwide FIFA ban after playing matches in Europe despite registration with Fulham.

**1979**

28 MARCH FIFA ban is lifted.
16 NOVEMBER Signs for Hibernian, leaving Fulham.
OCTOBER Manchester United refuse Best a testimonial.

**1980**

13 APRIL Signs to play for the San Jose Earthquakes in the NASL.
11 OCTOBER Plays his final game for Hibernian, at home against Falkirk.

**1981**

6 FEBRUARY Best's son Calum is born in San Jose.
19 AUGUST Plays his last ever game in the NASL for San Jose Earthquakes against the Vancouver Whitecaps, losing 1-3.

**1982**

NOVEMBER Declared bankrupt.

**1983**

24 MARCH Signs for AFC Bournemouth.
7 MAY Makes his final league appearance in a home game against Wigan Athletic.
3 JULY Plays briefly for the Brisbane Lions in Australia.

**1984**

3 NOVEMBER Charged with a drink driving offence.

**1985**

8 FEBRUARY Released from prison after serving eight weeks.

**1987**

DECEMBER The Irish FA refuse to grant Best a testimonial game.

**1988**

11 JANUARY Tribute programme, 'Best Intentions', is screened on Ulster Television.
8 AUGUST A testimonial organised by friends attracts 20,000 people in Belfast and raises £75,000 to help stave off bankruptcy.

**1990**

19 SEPTEMBER Best's infamous appearance on the Wogan Show.

**1995**

24 JULY Marries Alex Pursey, aged 23, at Chelsea Town Hall, London.

**1996**

22 MAY Best's 50th birthday is celebrated by an entire evening's viewing on BBC2.

**2000**

23 JANUARY Receives a unique services to football award from the Football Writers' Association.
9 MARCH Rushed to hospital with suspected liver failure.
13 APRIL Leaves hospital after almost five weeks.

**2001**

20 MAY Named the top Manchester footballer of the past fifty years by a *Manchester Evening News* Sunday Pink Panel.
13 DECEMBER Presented with an honorary degree from Queen's University in Belfast.

**2002**

3 APRIL Awarded the freedom of Castlereagh, the area of east Belfast where Best grew up.
30 JULY Goes into hospital for a 10-hour liver transplant operation.
8 DECEMBER BBC Sports Personality of the Year gives Best the lifetime achievement award.

**2003**

8 MARCH The subject of 'This Is Your Life' for the second time.

**2004**

2 FEBRUARY Receives a 20-month ban for drink driving.
14 APRIL Best is divorced by his wife Alex after nine years of marriage.

**2005**

1 OCTOBER Admitted to Cromwell Hospital with flu-like symptoms.
25 NOVEMBER George Best dies.

## Picture Credits

Every effort has been made to trace or contact all copyright holders. The publishers would be pleased to rectify any errors brought to their notice at the earliest opportunity.

**P1** Dick Green; **2** EMPICS; **4–5** L'Equipe / Offside; **7** Manchester United plc / Getty Images; **28** Getty Images; **29–31** POPPERFOTO; **32–3** Getty Images; **34–5** POPPERFOTO; **36** EMPICS; **37** Dick Green; **38** Getty Images; **39–41** POPPERFOTO; **42–3** Dick Green; **44–5** Getty Images; **46–7** Dick Green; **48** EMPICS; **49** Getty Images; **50–1** Action Images / MSI; **52** POPPERFOTO; **54** EMPICS; **55** Action Images / MSI; **56–7** Getty Images; **58–61** Dick Green; **62** (top) Action Images / MSI; (bottom) Getty Images; **63** Unknown; **65** Dick Green; **66–7** EMPICS; **68** Getty Images; **69** EMPICS; **70–71** Getty Images; **72–3** EMPICS; **74–77** Dick Green; **78–9** Action Images / MSI; **80–81** EMPICS; **82–3** Dick Green; **84** Action Images / MSI; **85** POPPERFOTO; **86–7** EMPICS; **88** Action Images / MSI; **89** L'Equipe / Offside; **90** Action Images; **91** Corbis; **92** EMPICS; **93** Getty Images; **94–5** Dick Green; **96** Action Images / MSI; **97–8** Getty Images; **99** EMPICS; **100** Getty Images; **100–1** POPPERFOTO; **102–3** (top) Getty Images; **103** (bottom) Sporting Pictures UK / Action Images; **104–5** Getty Images; **106–7** POPPERFOTO; **108–9** Roger Bamber; **110** Getty Images; **111** AP Photo / Peter Morrison / EMPICS **112** AP Photo / Jon Super / EMPICS **113** Phil Noble / PA / EMPICS; **114** Matthew Roberts / Reuters / Corbis; **115** Giampiero Sposito / Reuters / Corbis; **116–117** Reuters; **120** EMPICS.

First published in Great Britain in 2005 by Weidenfeld & Nicolson
10 9 8 7 6 5 4 3 2 1

Text copyright © David Meek and Sir Alex Ferguson 2005
Design and layout © Weidenfeld & Nicolson 2005

Design director: David Rowley
Designed by Grade Design Consultants
Design assistance by Justin Hunt
Colour reproduction by DL Repro

Edited by Matt Lowing
Editorial by Jennie Condell
Picture Research by Brónagh Woods

ISBN-13   978 0 297 84439 6
ISBN-10   0 297 84439 3

Printed and bound in Great Britain by Bath Press.

Weidenfeld & Nicolson
The Orion Publishing Group Ltd
Wellington House
125 Strand
London WC2R 0BB

The Orion Publishing Group's policy is to use papers that are natural, renewable and recyclable products and made from wood grown in sustainable forests. The logging and manufacturing processes are expected to conform to the environmental regulations of the country of origin.

**David Meek** was a sports journalist at the *Manchester Evening News* for 37 years, which placed him in a unique position to watch the young George Best develop into a footballing superstar. He now works for Manchester United Media and has a close association with the club. His previous titles include *Manchester United's Greatest 100 Players* (2004), *Manchester United in Europe* (2001) and *The Unique Treble* (2000), which he co-wrote with Manchester United manager Sir Alex Ferguson.

**Sir Alex Ferguson** is the most successful Manchester United manager of all time, guiding the club to eight Premiership titles, the European Cup-Winners' Cup (1990–1), five FA Cups, one Supercup and one League Cup as well as the Champions League in 1998–9 to complete a unique treble. Sir Alex was knighted in 1999.

**Page 1** George Best, aged two, playing outside his family home in Burren Way on the Cregagh Estate, Belfast.
**Page 2** A young Best in his early days at Manchester United.
**Page 4-5** George Best in April 1969 at the height of his success, after he had been named European Footballer of the Year.